ORDINARY TIME

FINDING HOLINESS IN EVERYDAY LIFE

D1713908

FR. MIKE SCHMITZ

ASCENSION

West Chester, Pennsylvania

Ascension
PO Box 1990
West Chester, PA 19380
1-800-376-0520

ascensionpress.com
Cover design: James Kegley

Printed in the United States of America
23 24 25 26 27 5 4 3 2 1

ISBN 978-1-954882-00-3 (trade book)
ISBN 978-1-954882-01-0 (e-book)

CONTENTS

WELCOME TO THE SUNDAY HOMILIES WITH FR. MIKE SCHMITZ COLLECTION

Each booklet in this series has been created to invite Catholics to grow closer to God through reflections from Fr. Mike.

These booklets are short and relatable, with features that will help you apply what you read to your own life.

Quotes and Bible verses throughout the booklets will help you zero in on the key points.

Questions after each section prompt you to reflect and help you to dive deeper into the topic being presented. We recommend that you pray or journal with these questions as you make connections to your everyday life. (They also make great prompts for small group discussion, while keeping in mind that not everyone in your group may feel comfortable answering those of a more personal nature.)

Meditations are provided after each reflection to help you take the topic directly into prayer. We recommend setting aside some time after each chapter to read the meditation and pray or journal with it.

Each reflection ends with a challenge to put what you have learned into action. These challenges invite you to enter into prayer, serve others, make a resolution for the week, and more.

It is our sincere hope **The Sunday Homilies with Fr. Mike Schmitz Collection** helps you along the way in your journey toward holiness. May God bless you!

*Note: This booklet is adapted from a series of homilies given by Fr. Mike Schmitz.

CHAPTER 1

DRIFTING

One theory among experts is that the Polynesian islands were populated by people who had drifted across the Pacific on rafts from South America. In 1947, a Norwegian explorer named Thor Heyerdahl decided to re-create their journey. He and his team built a raft out of the materials that these travelers would have used. After 101 days and 4,300 miles of drifting across the ocean, Heyerdahl and his companions finally arrived at the Polynesian Islands. This is the problem with drifting: sometimes it works.

THE KON-TIKI EXPEDITION

Led by Norwegian writer and explorer Thor Heyerdahl in 1947, the Kon-Tiki expedition journeyed across the Pacific Ocean from South America to the Polynesian islands.

Many people drift through their lives. They might have a vague idea of where they want to go but no plan on how to get there. They might say, "Plan? Are you kidding? I'm too busy!" So they are just drifting, hoping they will end up where they want to go without having a vision for how they will get there.

The Church's liturgical calendar gives us the beautiful seasons of Advent, Lent, Christmas, and Easter that help us focus our spiritual life on a specific event or goal—like growing in a particular sacrifice or practice of prayer. During Ordinary Time, though, we tend to just drift. We don't have a plan, a vision, or a destination. We just go through the motions.

But what if we chose to live Ordinary Time in an extraordinary way? What if we make the choice *not* to drift but to grow in our faith?

A VISION FOR YOUR LIFE

If we want to live an extraordinary life, we need three things: a destination, a plan, and a will.

The Gospel of Mark, chapter 10, presents us with the story of the rich young man, who seems to have a vision for his life and a desired destination. He approaches Jesus with a question: "Good Teacher, what must I do to inherit eternal life?" (Mark 10:17). In essence, Jesus responds, "Do you really want eternal life? Do you really want to do what you need to do to get there?"

In the book of Proverbs, the Lord says, "Without a vision the people lose restraint" (Proverbs 29:18, NAB). Now, the Israelites are God's chosen people. He has revealed his law to them and claimed them as his own … but they are dying. Why? Because they do not have a "vision"; they do not have a clear plan to reach their destination. Though the Lord chose them and revealed himself to them, they turned away from him—and became lost.

Like the Israelites, if we want to move forward, we need to know where we are going and have a vision to get there.

If we want to live an extraordinary life, we need three things: a destination, a plan, and a will.

In five years, what do you want to be true about your life?

First, what do you want to be true about your character? What kind of person do you want to be? Do you want to be someone others can count on? Do you want to be more *selfless* than *selfish*?

Second, what do you want to be true about your relationships—with your parents and siblings, with your friends, and with your spouse? Will you want them to know that you love them even more than you do today?

And finally, what do you want to be true about your relationship with God? Do you want your relationship with him to be more alive, intimate, and powerful?

YOUR VISION OR GOD'S VISION?

About a year ago, I met a man who seemed to have a clear idea of what he wanted his life to look like. In high school and college, he did his absolute best. After college, he married his college sweetheart and had a couple of children. He is a decent dad, a good husband, and an incredible businessman. He started and owns a company that has grown to have factories in multiple countries around the world, and he is a multimillionaire.

He looked kind of like the rich young man in the Gospel of Mark—a good man who had a vision for his life. In essence, the rich young man tells Jesus, "Here's the vision I have for my life. I want to be the kind of person who obeys the commandments. I want to be a good man. I want to go to heaven by doing good things."

But then Jesus flips things around, saying, "OK, that is *your* vision. Now let me tell you *my* vision of what your life could look like." He says, "Go, sell what you have, and give to the poor, and you will have treasure in heaven; and come, follow me" (Mark 10:21).

By following God's plan, we get more freedom.

While the rich young man had a fairly good vision for his life—being a good person by following the commandments—it ran up against Jesus' vision, which completely blew it out of the water. He wanted to be a decent guy in a small town in Israel, but Jesus said, "Actually, I want you to follow me as one of my disciples."

Imagine if this man had said yes. He would have become an incredible, holy person. He would have been brought into one of the most tight-knit brotherhoods that this world has ever seen. And he would have been able not only to share the mission of Jesus, but to actually be *friends* with him.

The crazy thing is that he walked away from Jesus. He decided that he wanted his vision more than he wanted Jesus' vision. Why? Maybe he simply didn't want to give up his riches, or maybe he didn't know if he could trust Jesus' vision because he wasn't sure where it would take him.

A few years ago, the successful businessman I mentioned earlier read a book that talked about how Jesus has a God-shaped vision for your life, a plan that is bigger than the one you have for yourself. As he continued reading, he came to realize, "I don't want *my* vision anymore. I want more."

This man has discovered that God's vision for his life isn't for him to be a *decent* husband and father but an *incredible* husband and father. To that end, he decided to sell his company. In addition to becoming an incredible family man, he believes God is calling him to spread the gospel to others. He has let go of his vision of who he wanted to be to seek who God wants him to be.

When we say yes to God's vision for our life, we trade in a less significant life for one of greater significance—and one that is more joyful. By following God's plan, we get more freedom, less selfishness, more generosity, and more wisdom.

MAKING A PLAN

You need a vision, but you also need a plan.

As the book of Wisdom says, "I prayed, and prudence was given [to] me" (Wisdom 7:7, NAB). Prudence means that we make a plan when we have a vision. Prudence asks, "If I want certain things to be true about my life in five years, what needs to change now so that those things can be true in five years?"

A vision without a plan is just a dream. Am I willing to have a plan, or am I just drifting through life, hoping that it all works out in the end? Do I think I am going to arrive in heaven without a plan to get there?

One of my heroes is the German Lutheran pastor Dietrich Bonhoeffer (1906–1945).[1] Now he was a man who had a passionate vision for his life. He came from a fairly wealthy family, and he was an incredible genius. He believed God was calling him to ministry, so he studied theology and became a pastor. He had a vision for his life, developed a plan, and followed it.

As he was living out his plan, he encountered Jesus. He was just like the rich young man whom Jesus asked, "Are you willing to set aside your vision and embrace mine?" Dietrich said yes, realizing that Jesus was calling him not just to be a good man but to be in a deep friendship with him.

Dietrich decided that if he wanted to have deep friendship with the Lord, he needed to pray every day. So he would rise every morning at five a.m. and pray for at least an hour. Then he would exercise, shower, and begin his work in ministry for the day. He followed this plan every day of his life for two decades, knowing that God's vision for his life was to share the adventure and mission of Christ.

When Adolph Hitler came to power, Dietrich was one of the few Lutheran pastors who stood against him. He was warned repeatedly by the Nazis to stop opposing their policies, but he kept up his preaching. Finally, in 1943, he was arrested and thrown into prison. Even in prison, he would continue his plan of rising at five a.m. to pray and spend time with the Lord.

DIETRICH BONHOEFFER
1906–1945
German Lutheran pastor and theologian who was killed by the Nazis
for preaching against the regime.

Bonhoeffer's vision was not altered by his circumstances. Rather, it *flourished* in his circumstances because it was not determined by them. He had practiced this in peacetime so that when wartime broke out, he lived a heroic life by continuing to follow the plan. He was able to share the gospel with nearly every man in the prison because he knew the vision God had for his life. He had put it into his plan and lived it every day.

Like Dietrich Bonhoeffer, we need God's vision for our lives, but we also need to commit to a plan to put that vision into practice. We need to put it on the calendar because having a vision and a plan are only good intentions if we don't have the will to act on them.

NEXT STEPS

I would like to invite you to try something I have found helpful. Make a list of three things you want to be true about *your character* in five years, three things you want to be true about *your relationships* in five years, and three things you want to be true about *your relationship with God* in five years.

God is calling us to stop drifting through life and seek something greater.

After you make your list of three things you want to be true about your character, your relationships, and your relationship with God in five years, determine one thing you are going to change to get closer to that vision for your life.

God is calling us to stop drifting through life and seek something greater. By having God's vision for our lives, a plan we can follow, and the will and the courage to make a change to get there, we will be able to create the extraordinary life to which he is calling us.

REFLECT

If you are a "planner," what is it that you like about planning things? If not, what is it about planning that turns you off or that you find difficult?

We can be intentional about *certain parts* of our lives while not really being intentional about our life. For example, we might be intentional about our work but "accidental" about our spiritual life. Discuss the parts of your life where you live "on purpose," intentionally.

What are the main obstacles that get in the way of your living life "on purpose"?

Do you find it challenging to discover God's vision for your life? Discuss.

PRAY

As we learned in Proverbs, God's people perish for lack of vision (see Proverbs 29:18). If we want to avoid simply drifting along through life, our view of things must be transformed and become God's vision. This happens by first offering everything to him in prayer. Thankfully, the Lord's will for our lives is that we *see* him, *know* him, and *love* him, so that we can spend eternity with him!

The Lord wants to guide us in our relationships, our careers, and our entire lives. Regardless of how all of the specific details play out in our life's journey, God himself is always our ultimate guide and destination.

If our lives are centered on the Lord, we don't need to be afraid to ask him to convert our vision and reorient our direction when we feel lost or anxious. When we turn to God in prayer and ask him to show us where our vision is hazy, he will give us clarity. If we ask him to show us his face, we will have all the vision for our lives that we need!

As you enter into prayer now, set all of your hopes and plans for the future at the feet of Jesus, turn your gaze away from all of your concerns, and look to him. If you feel you are drifting through life, unsure of where you are headed, set your eyes on the Lord, and he will show you the way! He will give you the "vision" to head straight toward him.

ACT

What are three things that you want to be true about your character, your relationships, and your relationship with God in five years? What is one thing you can do in each of these areas this week that will be a step toward making this vision a reality? Write them down.

CHAPTER 2

NO WONDER

We live in a time when life is amazing—in terms of technology—but few people are happy. We complain about our smartphone not being the newest model or lacking certain features, but forget that it is remarkable that this technology even exists. After all, it was not that long ago that the only phones we had were connected to a cord that went into a wall. Or when we travel by plane, we complain about having to pay for our snacks or the speed of the inflight Internet connection, forgetting how amazing it is that we can fly to our destination at all.

Recently, I was taking a taxi in Philadelphia, and I asked the driver, "Is it tough driving a cab with so many aggressive drivers out there?" He replied, "I have been a cabbie for thirty years. But the drivers have gotten much worse over the past few years. They act like they own the road and everyone else is in their way."

Such road rage comes from a sense of entitlement. Likewise, the idea that we deserve free snacks or high-speed Internet on a plane comes from a sense of entitlement, as does the idea that our smartphones should be better, cheaper, have more features, etc. The root of so much of the pervasive sadness and joylessness in our culture is due to this misplaced sense of entitlement. This isn't merely characteristic of one particular generation or another—this is something that goes all the way back to the Bible.

ORDINARY TIME

In the Gospel of Mark, Peter says to Jesus, "We have left everything and followed you" (Mark 10:28). Immediately after this, James and John approach Jesus and say, "Teacher, we want you to do for us whatever we ask of you" (Mark 10:35). How much more entitled could you be, to ask that of God? But I love Jesus' response; he just says, "What do you want me to do for you?" (Mark 10:36). He just rolls with it.

We see a similar sense of entitlement in the parable of the prodigal son. The son goes to his father and, in effect, says, "Dad, I don't want to wait until you die to get my inheritance, so just give it to me now" (see Luke 15:12). I guarantee that everyone who was listening when Jesus presented this parable was thinking, "Wow, what a spoiled kid!" At times, though, don't all of us act entitled? Maybe not to the extent of the prodigal son, but it is ordinary for us to want—to expect—to live lives that are not ordinary.

To live an extraordinary life, we need three things: a vision, a plan to accomplish this vision, and a will to choose this vision when it really counts. But the most important thing is to ask: *Is my vision God's vision?*

Many of us are afraid that God's vision is for us to live ordinary lives—to be just another ordinary person surrounded by other ordinary people living ordinary lives. The big secret, though, is that those who walk through life as if everything is ordinary have at least one thing in common: They walk through life as if God isn't real. But if God isn't real, then everything is accidental. There is no plan. There is no vision or meaning behind anything.

THE UNIVERSALS

Without God, there is no objective morality; what is good and bad is only one's opinion. Everything is based on preference or what a society considers useful. Think about the ways in which our advancement in technology, biology, or even weaponry comes down to whether something works or not. Without God, there is no true beauty in the world—just some things we find attractive and others we find unattractive.

Without God, there is no true beauty in the world.

Since so many of us go through life as if God does not exist, it's no wonder that we feel entitled. It's no wonder that we're not grateful. It's no wonder that there is so little hope among many we know and love. It's no wonder that there's so little joy in this world. It's no wonder that so few are captivated by life. It's no wonder that so few of us are moved by others. It's no wonder that so many of us are bored and dissatisfied. It's no wonder that so many of us live ordinary lives. We live ordinary lives because there is no *wonder*.

EVERYTHING IS A MIRACLE

The reality is that this world doesn't owe us anything. God certainly doesn't owe us anything! It's not necessary that we exist. But the crazy thing is that none of us is an accident; each of us has been willed by God before we were born (see Jeremiah 1:5). God doesn't owe us anything, but we owe him our very life. We need to repeat this truth every day.

If we have just randomly been brought into existence by the universe, then our lives have no meaning. But if God exists and we have been created by him, then our lives are full of meaning. The fact that we exist is a gift.

So why do we go through life without a sense of wonder? The universe didn't have to exist, but there is something rather than nothing. Do you ever wonder at yourself, at the reality that you can hold up your hand or move your body just by willing it? Do you ever wonder that you can open your eyes every morning and see the world? We should have gratitude and joy in these things.

God doesn't owe us anything, but we owe him our very life.

G. K. Chesterton, the famous English convert from atheism to the Catholic Faith, writes, "I would maintain that thanks are the highest form of thought, and that gratitude is happiness doubled by wonder."[2] Gratitude recognizes that we have gifts, while wonder recognizes that we don't have to have them. Chesterton goes on to say, "When we were children, we were grateful to those who filled our stockings at Christmas time. Why are we not grateful to God for filling our stockings with legs?"[3]

If there were no God, then everything would be an accident. But if God is real, then the opposite is also true. Everything that exists is a miracle. Every person is extraordinary. There is a great quote attributed to Albert Einstein: "There are only two ways to live your life. One is as though nothing is a miracle. The other is as though everything is a miracle." So why don't we expect miracles?

Wonder leads to gratitude, and gratitude leads to generosity and joy. If you want to have a life filled with generosity and joy, if you want to live a life of service, you need wonder. Every time Jesus met someone, he treated them as if they were extraordinary. This is why he said, "For the Son of man also came not to be served but to serve, and to give his life as a ransom for many" (Mark 10:45). There are no *ordinary* people.

NO ORDINARY PEOPLE

Several years ago, my friend Jason Evert shared a story with me about my former bishop, Bishop Robert Brom (1938–2022). When Bishop Brom was consecrated bishop of the Diocese of Duluth in 1983, he went to Rome to meet Pope John Paul II. As he walked into the pope's office, John Paul said, "Bishop Brom, it's so good to see you again."

Surprised, Bishop Brom said, "I'm sorry, Holy Father, but we've never met before." John Paul replied, "No, we've met before. This is the second time we've met." Again, Bishop Brom said, "I'm sorry, Holy Father, we've never met. You must be mistaken." So John Paul let it go and moved on with the meeting.

Later that day, Monsignor Dziwisz, the pope's personal secretary, tracked Bishop Brom down and scolded him: "Never argue with the Holy Father." Monsignor Dziwisz continued, "When you were a seminarian here in Rome during the Second Vatican Council, you were coming out of the Church of the Gesù with three other American seminarians when Archbishop Wojtyla was walking in with three Polish seminarians. That's when you first met John Paul II."

Every encounter with another human being is an encounter with God himself.

Bishop Brom was shocked that the pope would remember such a brief encounter after two decades. Monsignor Dziwisz replied, "For John Paul, every encounter with another human being is an encounter with God himself, so he remembers everyone."

Every encounter with another human being is an encounter with God himself, so he remembers everyone. St. John Paul II was filled with wonder every time he met another human being. That is what it is to have an extraordinary life, filled with wonder, knowing that there are no ordinary people.

As C. S. Lewis writes, "There are no *ordinary* people. You have never talked to a mere mortal. Nations, cultures, arts, civilizations—these are mortal, and their life is to ours as the life of a gnat. But it is immortals whom we joke with, work with, marry, snub, and exploit."[4]

Throughout your entire life, you have only met extraordinary people! Therefore, if you want to live a life of generosity, joy, and service, you must start with wonder. You don't have to work harder. You don't have to serve more. You don't have to increase generosity or joy in your life. If you want to break out of an ordinary life and start living an extraordinary life, if you want to break out of just treating people like they're ordinary and start seeing the truth that there are no ordinary people, start with wonder.

C.S. LEWIS ON "ORDINARY" PEOPLE

"There are no *ordinary* people. You have never talked to a mere mortal. Nations, cultures, arts, civilizations—these are mortal, and their life is to ours as the life of a gnat. But it is immortals whom we joke with, work with, marry, snub, and exploit."

So it should not be surprising that those who go through life without God are filled with sadness. Since they believe that they are entitled to everything they have, everything begins to feel ordinary. Nothing means anything, so life becomes boring. They lack wonder.

If you want to have an extraordinary life with extraordinary people, doing extraordinary things, have wonder. This leads to gratitude, generosity, joy, and service.

REFLECT

Who is the most interesting person you have met? What made him or her interesting?

Describe a time when you felt "entitled." Were you justified in your sense of entitlement or not?

How would you respond to the statements that "the world does not owe you anything" and "God does not owe you anything"?

Discuss when an experience of God awakened a sense of wonder in your life.

PRAY

When a bishop administers Confirmation, he begs the Holy Spirit to fill those who are receiving this sacrament with a "spirit of wonder and awe" in the Lord's presence. This is what God wants for each of us—to be filled with wonder and awe at every moment, because we are *always* in his presence!

Our challenge is to use moments of boredom, the mundane, and the annoying as opportunities to draw closer to God. When we do that, every day becomes filled with new wonder and joy. There are no "throwaway moments" with God. There is not one minute of the day when the Lord is not present, wanting to infuse each of us with his grace and wonder. We just need to *seek him* out.

So as you enter into prayer today, ask God to open your eyes to the reality that he is always right there with you. Ask him to fill your life with the "spirit of wonder and awe," moment by moment, prayer by prayer. If you do this, you will discover wonder in your best and worst moments, in your successes and failures, and during times of comfort and struggle—the wonder that comes from God's presence in your life.

ACT

Commit to cultivating wonder in your life this week. Every day, break out of the "ordinary" and seek wonder, gratitude, and an extraordinary life.

CHAPTER 3

DO IT NOW

Recently, I was looking through some old yearbooks. One of the funny things about yearbooks is what could be called the "superlatives" voting section—you know, where students get to vote on which classmate is the best athlete, the most artistic, the most intellectual, or the funniest.

Nearly all of these "yearbook superlatives" are based on something someone has already done. But there is one superlative in almost every high school yearbook that is not based on what a person has done but on his *potential*: the most likely to succeed.

Now, a person can fail to live up to his or her potential. For example, a standout high school athlete might have the potential to be a star in college—and even make it to the pros—but then fizzles out for one reason or another.

Sometimes, not living up to one's potential can simply be due to a lack of opportunity.

GREAT POTENTIAL

The people of Israel, because they were chosen by God, had an incredible amount of potential. Out of all the nations, God chose Israel to be his special possession. So they had great potential.

Due to the people's rebellion against the Lord, though, Israel was divided into northern and southern kingdoms. In the eighth century BC, the northern kingdom was invaded and exiled by the Assyrians. And the southern kingdom was invaded and sent into exile by the Babylonians in the sixth century BC. God's chosen people were no longer in Jerusalem. They no longer had the Temple. They no longer had their homes. Due to their sins, they did not live up to their potential.

In the book of Jeremiah, chapter 29, the Lord, in effect, says to his people: "You are going to be taken from your home to this far-off place because of your rebellion against me. But you still have potential. So when you arrive in Babylon, build houses to dwell in. Plant gardens. Eat the fruits. Marry and have children. Find wives for your sons and husbands for your daughters."

Basically, God is telling them, "I know this situation is not ideal, but you still have the potential to live now."

JEREMIAH'S LETTERS TO THE EXILES IN BABYLON

"Thus says the LORD of hosts, the God of Israel, to all the exiles whom I have sent into exile from Jerusalem to Babylon: Build houses and live in them; plant gardens and eat their produce. Take wives and have sons and daughters; take wives for your sons, and give your daughters in marriage, that they may bear sons and daughters; multiply there, and do not decrease. But seek the welfare of the city where I have sent you into exile, and pray to the LORD on its behalf, for in its welfare you will find your welfare" (Jeremiah 29:4–7).

As baptized Christians, we have been given the gift of the Holy Spirit. We have been given full access to the Father, full access to the throne of grace that is spoken of in the letter to the Hebrews, full access to mercy. As a Christian, you have the same potential for holiness as any of the saints.

The difference between the saints and us is not in our potential. It is not in the particular gifts we have been given. The only difference between the saints and us is that *they took action*. They saw their potential, and they lived it out heroically through the help of God's grace. Imagine if someone gave the eulogy at your funeral and said, "She had a lot of potential—and she died with a lot of potential." How tragic it would be if your tombstone reads, "He had a lot of potential."

You have the same potential for holiness as any of the saints.

The difference between an ordinary and an extraordinary life lies in deciding to use your potential *now*. Every person, every Christian you have ever met, has the potential to be holy, to be a saint, to live an extraordinary life. But many choose to live an ordinary life because it is easier—it is "ordinary"—to live unchanged. It is extraordinary to say, "I am going to change. I am going to do it *now*. I am going to use my potential *now*."

MAKE A CHANGE

Recently, I heard a presentation in which the speaker pointed out that humans are the only creatures on the planet that can *change*. Have you ever thought about that? Animals can grow and adapt to their environment, but they can't decide to change. Only you and I can do that, because only you and I have been created in God's image and likeness—that is, with reason and free will.

Animals can't change. But we can. We have personal agency. We can choose to change or not, either later or now. What is remarkable, though, is that so few of us are actually willing to change.

Many of us just drift through life, hoping that we will simply arrive at somewhere good. But the only way to make a change in our life is by making positive choices. Our decisions determine our destiny, so if we are reluctant to make a choice, we are not really serious about our destiny.

Remember, if God has a vision for our lives, we can either make decisions for it or put them off until later. But the truth is that personal *agency*— our ability to make a choice—is connected to personal *responsibility*. And there is only one person who is responsible for whether you get to your destination or if you fail—you. God has given you the potential, through his grace, to get where you need to go. Even if you fail at times, you can get back up through confession and receive an abundance of his grace.

Taking responsibility means that if I did something terrible or someone did something terrible to me, even accidentally, I say, "In this moment, I have the ability to respond." In these types of situations, we can ask, "What's the best way for me to respond here? What can I do with my potential? How can I act now rather than later?"

In the Gospel, the blind man Bartimaeus hears that Jesus is passing by, and he immediately cries out to him. He acts *now*. He doesn't wait. Though people tell him to be quiet, he calls out all the more because this is his one shot to see Jesus as he is passing by (see Mark 10:46–52).

Finally, Jesus responds, telling the people to bring Bartimaeus to him. I love how Mark describes this: He says that Bartimaeus "threw aside" his cloak. He didn't place it to the side. He sprang to his feet. This is not a guy who was taking his time to get to Jesus.

Jesus says, "What do you want me to do for you?" And the blind man replies, "Master, I want to see" (see Mark 10:51). Later? No, *now*. It's all about now.

TWO OPTIONS

In the end, we have two options: We can let our lives can be defined by their potential or by our choices now.

There are three words that I ask you to inscribe on your heart: *Do it now.*

When it comes to something you could do later, do it now. When it comes to something that lines up with the vision that God placed in your heart, do it now. The difference between a person who dies with potential and one who dies as a saint is that the saint does what they need to do *now*. The saint does not put things off until later.

All of us have experienced these options. When you got ready for Mass on Sunday, maybe you stepped over a pile of clothes in your room that you noticed days before and said, "I should wash those. Well, I'll do it later." On Sunday, they were still there. Why? Because you had a chance to wash your clothes earlier in the week, but you chose to do it later.

Maybe you were hungry, and when you went to the cupboard to get a bowl for your cereal, there weren't any because they were all stacked up in the sink waiting to be washed. Every day of that week, instead of cleaning your bowl after using it, you decided to do it later. So you were stuck without a clean bowl.

So why do we procrastinate? People give various answers: "I procrastinate because I'm afraid to make a choice. I'm afraid of missing out. I like to keep my options open. I want to do it perfectly when I have more time."

Now, we can get away with putting things off for a while. But the problem with living with "later" as our theme song is that we will just be living an ordinary life. We will not be getting any closer to our destiny, to making the changes that God wants to make in our life. So again, I say: When it comes to doing something later or now, do it now. Do it now with grace. Do what you need to do when you first get the chance to do it.

Three words that I ask you to inscribe on your heart: *Do it now.*

Recently, I was talking with a young man who said that his coworkers were in awe of how great an employee he was. Why? Because he did what he needed to do *when* he needed to do it! For example, when it was time to make a call to a client, he made the call. When it was time to send out a letter, he sent out the letter. He did things *now.*

Basically, his coworkers and his employer were praising this man simply because he was willing to do the baseline. He had the opportunity to do things now or later—and he chose to do them in the moment. He was just doing the ordinary, but his coworkers saw this as something extraordinary.

It's not that difficult. As St. Francis of Assisi has been quoted as saying, "Start by doing what's necessary; then do what's possible; and suddenly you are doing the impossible."

So begin by doing what is necessary. Do it *now.* Then do the possible *now.* Soon, you will be doing the extraordinary *now.* This is the difference between an ordinary and an extraordinary life. This is the difference between someone who dies full of potential and someone who dies as a saint.

It comes down to a simple decision: I can do it *later,* or I can do it *now.*

REFLECT

Do you struggle with procrastination in one area more than another? Why do you think this is?

Do you like or dislike change? Why do you think this is? Discuss an example of a painful change that you appreciated after the fact.

Do you find it easy or difficult to make decisions? Discuss some reasons why this might be the case. What do you think about the statement "decision determines our destiny"?

Discuss how personal agency is connected to personal responsibility.

PRAY

It is crazy, but even after a clear call to act immediately—"do it now"—we might find ourselves wanting another nudge, another quick reflection, another ... *something*... to spur us on more. The fact is, we don't need anything else. We just need *action*. We don't need additional reflection, discussion, or encouragement. We just need to do it *now.*

Of course, we need to pray and ask God what he wants us to
do, but Scripture reminds us that faith without works is dead
(see James 2:17). So we must put our prayer into action—and we
must give action to our prayer. The beauty of life in Christ is that
because we can offer our action to God as a prayer, we can act
and pray at the same time!

So...

Pray *now*. Call that person *now*. Clean your room *now*. Forgive that
person *now*. Pay that bill *now*. Right that wrong *now*. Read God's
Word *now*. Face that doubt *now*. Do all the dishes *now*. Feed the
hungry *now*. Get rid of that attachment *now*. Confess your sins
now. Whatever it is that you can do at this moment, *do it now*!

ACT

Write the phrase "Do it now" where you know you will see it every
day. This week, when you know that you need to do something—
and you could do it now or later—do it *now*.

CHAPTER 4
ASK, OFFER, ACCEPT

When I was a kid, my mom had my siblings and me join the local swim team. She wanted all of us to learn how to swim well because she was afraid of the water. So when I was six, I joined the Brainerd, Minnesota swim team, … and I stunk. I was *bad*. In fact, I was the slowest kid on the only swim team in town.

That's fine when you are six years old and the youngest. But then, when I turned seven, I was still the slowest kid on the team. Same at eight. Understandably, I wanted to quit many, many times!

Then something happened. I got better. I started winning. So I kept swimming, not because I suddenly liked swimming, but because I liked winning. I would have quit if I thought that no matter how hard I worked, it would be impossible for me to win.

YOU CAN BE A SAINT

Recently, I had the opportunity to visit with Catholic author and speaker Matthew Kelly. He shared with me the most commonly believed lie among Catholics—that holiness and sainthood are for others, not for me.

Many of us believe only bishops, priests, monks, nuns, and our grandmas need to be holy. We do not think holiness is for us. Ultimately, with this attitude, we are telling ourselves that "winning" in our faith is not possible for us. But the very reason the Church exists is to give God glory and to make saints.

If we buy into the lie that holiness is not for us, then we are saying that the Church doesn't work—which means that the grace of God it gives us through the sacraments doesn't work. We're saying that we have to be someone else in order to be saints.

> The very reason the Church exists is
> to give God glory and to make saints.

In recent years, Halloween has become the fastest growing holiday in the United States, with adults celebrating it as much as children. It wasn't that long ago that Halloween was just for kids to get dressed up and go trick or treating. But now, many adults get dressed up and go out as well. Maybe this is because they get to dress up and pretend to be someone else.

A friend of mine, Fr. Nick Nelson, and I were recently talking about different movies and television shows we like. At one point, he said, "If I had to be someone else, it would be Jason Bourne from *The Bourne Identity*." I loved how he said that. He didn't say, "If I *could choose* to be someone else …" but "If I *had* to be someone else …" Why? Because if he had a hundred lives, he would choose to be a priest in every single one of them. Fr. Nick understands that holiness is all about being himself, the person God created him to be, not being someone else.

ST. FRANCIS DE SALES

1567–1622

French Catholic priest who served as bishop of Geneva and wrote the influential spiritual work *Introduction to the Devout Life*

St. Francis de Sales was known as the "saint maker." When people met him, he showed them how they could be saints. He made it simple for them: "Be what you are and be that well." You do not need to be someone else. Be who you are—and be "you" well.

So, the question remains: Who are you?

In 1 John 3:2, we read, "Beloved, we are God's children now." This is the deepest truth about who you are. You are a son or daughter of God. You have been called to have a personal relationship with him.

> If we want to be a saint, we need to say yes to God and never stop saying yes.

A saint is someone who says yes to God and never stops saying yes. Even if we sin, we can say yes to God by going to confession. Even if we are away from the Church, we can say yes to God and return. Even if we find ourselves in a place we would not like to be, even when we are experiencing the worst day of our life, we can say yes to God. If we want to be a saint, we need to say yes to God and never stop saying yes.

How can you and I do this, starting right now? How can we start living like saints? How can we start racing to win, believing we can actually win today?

START TODAY

Here are two things you can do right now.

One, spend time with God every day. Take five minutes to read the Bible every day. You don't have to come up with your own Bible reading plan. You can look up the daily Mass readings online and read through them, letting the Holy Spirit speak to you through the words of Scripture. Then, write down one thing from your Bible reading that you want to carry with you into the day.

Often, the reason we are not running to win is that we keep God in a box. We keep him out of our everyday lives. We think, "I can never be a saint because a saint is someone who does holy things all day." We see our daily lives as ordinary and going to church as extraordinary, so we don't see every day as an opportunity for holiness. If we don't strive to be holy in our "ordinary time"—our daily life, our work or school life, and our family life—then no, we can't become saints. We can't run this race to win. But if we can sanctify every moment, then our entire lives can become sanctified.

Here is the second way you can start living like a saint right now. It is a secret from St. Francis de Sales. Three words: *ask*, *offer*, and *accept*. Throughout your day, *ask* God to be with you. Ask for his grace to be present in your life. Then, *offer* every moment to him. Give to him that time as a gift. Finally, resolve to *accept* whatever happens.

If you do this, you can become the saint God wants you to be. Again, this is not necessarily about spending more time in church doing "holy" things; it is about bringing the holy things into your ordinary time. When we do this, every ordinary moment is transformed into an extraordinary moment. Ordinary time becomes holy time.

Offer every moment up to God. My friend Fr. Ben is a great athlete. Ever since college, he prays before he goes out for a run or on a bike ride. He says, "God, I offer you this time. I offer you this run (or this bike ride). I offer you the pain that's going to be involved. It's my gift to you."

Maybe you have a meeting this week that you don't want to go to. Say, "God, I invite you to be with me in this meeting. Make it holy. I offer it to you as a sacrifice." When you offer something up to God, it changes an ordinary moment of your life into worship.

We had a surprise birthday party for my mom. After celebrating two Masses that morning, I drove three hours to the party. I was able to say, "Hi, Mom. Happy birthday. I love you." Then, forty-five minutes later, I had to drive back to Duluth. I said, "Bye, Mom. Happy birthday. I love you." During my six-hour round trip, I prayed, "God, I give this time to you. Make it a sacrifice." So I spent the entire time in the car in worship.

When you offer something up to God, it changes an ordinary moment of your life into worship.

Do you know what our main job in heaven will be? Worshipping God. If you can't bear to worship God for an hour on Sunday, heaven is not going to be your cup of tea. So make your ordinary time a time of worship simply by saying, "God, I give this moment to you. I resolve to accept whatever it is you want to do with this." This is the third part: *Accept* what God brings you in the moment.

If you do this with your ordinary time—if you *ask, offer,* and *accept* throughout the course of your day—you can be the saint God has made you to be. You are going to see change in your life—and be who you are.

When people struggle with habitual sins, there are several steps that come before the sin. For example, if one struggles with pornography, perhaps he goes on his computer or smartphone just to check email or log onto

Facebook, and it's a slippery slope from there. To stop a slide into looking at the wrong thing on the Internet, he could pray, "I have to check my email. God, be with me in this moment. I give you this time of checking my email as an offering to you." This can dictate where he goes from there. By entrusting this time to God, it is likely that he is going to stay away from anything that he doesn't want to offer to the Lord.

RUN TO WIN

After my siblings and I became swimmers, all of us eventually became triathletes. Our family vacations involved going to triathlons or marathons. There was an Ironman Triathlon we attended in the mountains of Penticton, British Columbia. An Ironman Triathlon consists of a 2.4-mile swim, a 112-mile bike ride, and a 26.2-mile marathon run. So it is an intense day. For the last five miles, you run through town, with people standing shoulder to shoulder along the road, cheering. Then, during the last hundred-meter stretch, there are bleachers on either side of the road and people in the stands.

Everyone starts the race at seven in the morning, and you have to finish the race by midnight. If you do not cross the finish line by midnight, you are disqualified. After your name, they write three letters: DNF. Did Not Finish.

One year, after everyone in my family had finished the race, we went back to the hotel, showered, and ate dinner. Then, around ten o'clock, we went back to the finish line to cheer on the remaining racers. This is an Ironman tradition.

At about 11:45 p.m., the announcer said, "There is someone out there right now. He is two miles out from the finish line. We've got to bring him in." The people around me who had just finished the race started jumping off the bleachers and tearing down Main Street to run this person in. My legs were tired, so I just sat there, cheering other people on. I thought, *There is no way this guy is going to run back-to-back seven-and-a-half-minute miles after he's been racing since 7:00 a.m., and he's not done yet. No way.*

Well, a couple minutes passed by, and it was about eight minutes from midnight. And the guy got on the mic and said, "He's under a mile away." My brother, sister, and I were freaking out, asking, "How is this even possible!?"

As it got closer to midnight, about 11:59, there was a dull roar in the back to the right of us that kept getting louder as it got closer. We looked down this hundred-meter stretch, and pretty soon, a guy burst out from around the corner. He was sprinting as fast as he possibly could, racing for the finish line. The incredible thing was that hundreds of other racers were running him in. They were running behind him, next to him, with him. The guy finished the race at 11:59:47, with thirteen seconds to spare.

Everyone was emotional at this incredible feat. But there is no way that guy could have done it if those other runners, who had already finished the race, hadn't run him in. He had nothing left to give. They couldn't run the race for him, but they could run with him. Because he wasn't running alone, he was able to do something impossible.

The communion of saints is like the runners who helped this guy cross the finish line. The saints, our brothers and sisters, have run ahead of us. They have finished the race. They have won the prize. They can't run *for* us, but they can run *with* us. And they do. As the letter to the Hebrews says, "We are surrounded by so great a cloud of witnesses" (Hebrews 12:1). These are all the people who have run the race—and won.

"We are surrounded by so great a cloud of witnesses."

—Hebrews 12:1

As followers of Jesus, we are surrounded by the saints. We are not alone. If you've been thinking, *There's no way I can run this race*, I'm inviting you right now to be what you are and be that well. You are a son or daughter of God. The secret to being what you are and being that well involves, in every moment, asking God to be present, offering him that moment, and resolving to accept whatever happens. That transforms ordinary time into sanctified time. That transforms your ordinary life into the life of a saint.

Every year, on the first of November, we celebrate the Solemnity of All Saints. I invite you to live each day as if All Saints' Day is *your* feast day. Live each day of your discipleship with Christ as a saint. You don't have to wait for tomorrow. You don't have to wait for a holy hour. You don't have to wait for anything. In this moment, *ask, offer*, and *accept*. Make the ordinary time in your life into extraordinary, sanctified time. That's the life of a saint. Run to win.

REFLECT

Who is someone you know that you admire? What was it about them that you see as exceptional? Do you find some of the same characteristics or gifts in your own life?

Sainthood is about who our heart belongs to. *Ask, offer*, and *accept* is about orienting our heart toward God's will. Discuss some practical ways you can do this in your life.

Are there any times in your life that you find it more difficult than others to ask God to be present, offer him the moment, and resolve to accept the result? Discuss.

The communion of saints is real. Have you ever experienced the intercession of a saint in your life? How?

PRAY

In your prayer today, meditate on St. Francis de Sales' method to *ask*, *offer*, and *accept*. Though God is already with you in this moment, your act of *asking* him to be with you is your way of acknowledging his presence. Whether you are aware of him or not, the Lord is always with you—so *ask* him to *make you aware* of his presence now.

Next, *offer* this moment of prayer to him. Whatever the state of your mind, heart, and emotions, offer it to him. If you are distracted, hungry, grumpy, tired, or ecstatic, offer it to him. Don't try to force your feelings or pretend things are different from how they are. Offer him the *actual* moment you are experiencing. This is the beauty of having a relationship with Jesus in prayer— you don't need to fake anything. He knows you; he knows where you are and what you are going through. So offer him your "now," as it is.

Then, *accept* whatever happens next. Perhaps you ask and offer, and then your phone rings, or a child comes running in and needs you. Accept that! Otherwise, you are trying to control what happens, and this doesn't work well in life. If you've asked God to be present and offered him this present moment, then he has heard your prayer. Now, the only thing that remains is for *you* to accept what happens next.

Once you begin "asking, offering, and accepting," seek to make
this practice consistent in your prayer. It is easy to forget to do
this. As you enter into prayer in *this* moment, don't focus on all
the times you forgot to ask, offer, and accept in the past. Focus on
asking, offering, and accepting *now*.

ACT ///

When we ask God into every moment, we are asking him to
sanctify each moment. When we offer God every moment, every
moment becomes worship. When we accept what God brings us
in every moment, we are saying "your will be done." This week,
go past last week's "do it now" plan and seek to "ask, offer, and
accept" at least five times each day.

CHAPTER 5
LAST TEN PERCENT

Sacrifice is a part of daily life.

We might sacrifice sleep to spend more time with our friends. We might sacrifice spending time with our friends to study or work. Or we might sacrifice going to our favorite restaurant because our friends want to eat somewhere else. Sacrifices don't have to be a big deal.

Sometimes we don't even think twice about this. Have you ever been so passionate about something, so fixated on a goal, that you didn't even think twice about making a sacrifice to get to that goal? No one had to tell you, "Don't do this. Start doing that." You were already willing to give up anything to get there. You were already doing it.

It is a natural part of life to trade things of lesser value for things of greater value, to trade things that are ordinary for those that are extraordinary.

FIRSTFRUITS

Recently, I was meeting with a couple preparing for marriage. The groom spoke about how he gave to the Church and charity by tithing, which usually means giving ten percent of your income, the firstfruits. In his case, though, he gave ten percent of his income *after* he paid his rent, insurance, and taxes; in other words, he was giving what was left over.

It sounded like he was raised like I was. My parents would give each of us six kids a quarter to put in the collection basket at Mass. They were trying to teach us that it's a good thing to give to the Church. The problem is that we started out with a quarter and stayed there. Since we put a quarter in the basket as children, we now put in a dollar as adults.

This man and his fiancée decided that, after they were married, they would give their firstfruits, ten percent, from the beginning. The concept of tithing comes right from the Old Testament (see Genesis 14:18–20; Genesis 28:16–22; Deuteronomy 14:22–29). If you were a farmer, you would leave ten percent of your field unharvested so that the poor could come and eat from it. If you raised fig or olive trees or grew grapes, when you would pick the figs, olives, and grapes, you wouldn't go back for those that fell on the ground because they were for the poor. This was a tithe to the Lord.

In Israel, the idea of the tithe, of giving one's firstfruits, also meant that you brought it to the Temple. Those who were not farmers or who didn't grow grapes, figs, or olives would take the first ten percent of their earnings, go to the Temple, and purchase an animal to offer as a sacrifice.

In the Bible, sacrifice is always connected to worship. In fact, in all religions throughout history, sacrifice is the heart of worship. This involves taking something precious to us and handing it over to God. This handing over presupposes that it is withdrawn from our use.

We take what is ordinary, and we give it to God. He asks for the first ten percent of our stuff. He asks for our time. He asks us to give up our time on the Sabbath day, to not use it for ourselves, but to just give it so we have some freedom. We just hand it over; we surrender that time.

The truth is that few things reveal the truth of where our hearts are like our stuff or our time. God doesn't need an animal burning on an altar. He is the God of the universe. He is the creator and sustainer of everything that exists. Everything belongs to him. But we give him our hearts by offering him ordinary things to which they are connected and they become sacred. They become extraordinary.

GIVE IT ALL

Right before the scene in Mark's Gospel when the poor widow gives her donation, one of the scribes approaches Jesus and asks, "Which commandment is the first of all?" (Mark 12:28). Jesus answers, "You shall love the Lord your God with all your heart, and with all your soul, and with all your mind, and with all your strength. ... You shall love your neighbor as yourself" (Mark 12:30–31). And the scribe says, "You are right, Teacher ... to love him with all the heart, and with all the understanding, and with all the strength, and to love one's neighbor as oneself, is much more than all whole burnt offerings and sacrifices" (Mark 12:32–33).

In the Bible, the phrase "burnt offering" is very specific because some offerings were not entirely destroyed. A sin offering, for example, was when a person would take a goat to the priest, who would slaughter it, put some of its fat and its kidneys on the altar, and then burn them up. The meat of the rest of the animal would go to the priest. With a burnt offering (also known as a holocaust offering), however, the entire animal would be sacrificed.

In the Old Testament, people were commanded to give God ten percent. Here, Jesus says that God just asked for your first ten percent to get to your heart. Your things and your time are connected to your heart, so to love the Lord your God with all your heart, mind, soul, and strength is worth more than all burnt offerings.

SURPLUS OR SUBSTANCE?

In the Gospel of Mark, we see Jesus is standing outside of the treasury, watching as wealthy people give large sums of money, while a poor widow comes and puts in two copper coins, which are basically worth a penny. Jesus says that she put in more than everyone else because they gave from their surplus but she gave all she had to God.

This is what it comes down to. There are two ways to live. You can live out of your surplus or out of your substance. There are two ways to worship. You can worship out of your surplus, or you can worship out of your substance.

THE WIDOW'S OFFERING

"And he sat down opposite the treasury, and watched the multitude putting money into the treasury. Many rich people put in large sums. And a poor widow came, and put in two copper coins, which make a penny. And he called his disciples to him, and said to them, 'Truly, I say to you, this poor widow has put in more than all those who are contributing to the treasury. For they all contributed out of their abundance; but she out of her poverty has put in everything she had, her whole living'" (Mark 12:41–44).

Many of us tend to live and worship out of our surplus. We look at our lives and see a few holy things sprinkled around them. But Jesus says, "I want a different ten percent. Not the *first* ten percent but something else. I want the *last* ten percent." It is giving that last ten percent—in other words, our entire hearts—that makes us saints.

Have you heard the story of the chicken and the pig? The chicken and the pig are walking down a country lane, and the chicken says to the pig, "Farmer Johnson has been so good to us. Let's do something nice for him."

The pig looks at the chicken and says, "Well, what do you think we should do?"

And the chicken says, "I think we should give Farmer Johnson a great breakfast of ham and eggs."

The pig looks at the chicken and says, "Well, that's fine for you because you're merely involved, but I'd have to be fully committed."

And that is the difference. The difference of that last ten percent is the difference of being involved versus committed.

It is giving that last ten percent—in other words,
our entire hearts—that makes us saints.

In marriage, that last ten percent is critical. If you're not married, you don't dream of the day that you meet the love of your life, and that person looks you deep in the eyes and says, "I want to love you with ninety percent of my heart." Or the person looks at you and says, "Would you marry me? I would love to spend ninety percent of my life with you."

No one would desire that ninety percent. In marriage, that last ten percent is not the difference between a good marriage and a great marriage. The last ten percent is the difference between having an ordinary marriage and one that is extraordinary.

Think of Jesus. He loves you with one hundred percent of his heart, one hundred percent of the time.

Imagine if he loved us only ninety percent. God, who made everything, became one of us. He walked the earth. He preached, healed people, and raised the dead. Then came the Last Supper, then the garden at Gethsemane. Soldiers arrested him, scourged him, and put a crown of thorns on his head. He was condemned, carried the cross to Golgotha, and was nailed to it. The crowd shouts at him, "If you're the Son of God, come down off the cross, and we will believe you."

What if, at that point, Jesus said, "OK, I'm done"?

This is the difference. This is the difference between salvation and heaven remaining closed. That last ten percent of Jesus' gift makes all the difference. It is the difference between Jesus and Judas.

Think about that. Judas was a chosen apostle. He followed Jesus for three years. He followed him almost to the very end—and then he stopped. He did not give Jesus his last ten percent.

So will we give Jesus our last ten percent or not?

If God only has access to our surplus, then the only part of us that can be transformed is the extra stuff, not the substance of our lives.

I think that the idea of giving God our last ten percent scares many of us. We think, *What is that going to mean for my life? How much more can I possibly give to the Lord?* So we try to hold on to the last ten percent.

The first book of Kings tells the story of Elijah and the widow of Zarephath (see 1 Kings 17:8–16). The story begins in the middle of a drought. Elijah goes up to a woman he doesn't know and asks for a cup of water.

My first thought is, *There's a drought. She probably doesn't have any water.* But she's fine with the request.

Elijah then asks her for a little biscuit or a cake. Who does he think he is?

The woman tells him that she has fallen on hard times. She only has a little oil and some flour left, and she is picking up sticks to make a fire to bake a cake for her and her son. She tells the prophet that after they eat it, they will die.

Elijah doesn't seem to pay attention to her words. He repeats his request. *What is going on?* But the woman does what he asks.

The remarkable thing is that this poor widow gives Elijah the *last ten percent* of all she has.

What if she had held onto it? What if he she had made her son and herself a little cake instead? They would have died a day later. But because she was willing to offer God the last ten percent, she received so much more back than she ever possibly could have imagined.

This is why Pope Benedict says that in Christ, God reveals that the goal of worship is not destruction but divinization.[5] The goal of sacrifice is transformation. What you give up in your life becomes transformed in God's hands. It is lifted up.

This is what happens when we go to Mass. We offer "ordinary stuff." We offer God bread and wine—and what happens? It is not destroyed but becomes transformed into the Body, Blood, Soul, and Divinity of his Son Jesus. He takes the ordinary and makes it extraordinary. He makes it sacred.

ORDINARY MADE EXTRAORDINARY

So what does giving your last ten percent look like for you?

After I preached on this topic, a woman approached me and said, "Father, when you say give the last ten percent—one hundred percent—you know what word goes through my head: *burnout*." Let's look at this.

Remember St. Francis de Sales' secret to holiness, to becoming a saint? It is to let God have our "ordinary stuff" by *asking, offering,* and *accepting.* In every situation, *ask* God to be present. Then, in that moment, say, "God, I *offer* you this moment as a gift. Make it a sacrifice. Make it worship." Then, resolve to *accept* whatever happens.

Today, here is what the last ten percent looked like for me. After celebrating Masses this morning, I went home and made lunch. It was a beautiful day, so I went outside to grill a steak. As I was grilling on this warm, sunny day, I said, "God, be with me right now. I give you this moment as a gift, and I resolve to accept whatever happens with this moment."

This is not a picture of burnout. It is picture of me taking the ordinary moments of life that I love for twenty minutes and saying, "God, be with me. Accept this as my sacrifice. I'm giving the ordinary stuff. Transform it, and I resolve to accept whatever happens."

After I finished my steak and a beer, I had twelve minutes until marriage prep. So I thought, *I'm going to lie down.* So I did. And I said, "God, be with me right now. I give you this time as I'm lying down, and I resolve to accept whatever you do with this time."

Then, when it was time to get up to the marriage prep meeting, I said, "God, be with me as I speak with this couple. I offer our time together up to you. And I resolve to accept whatever happens out of this."

See, giving the Lord our last ten percent does not lead to burnout. It leads to transformation.

If you have been trying to ask, offer, and accept, how do you know what your last ten percent really is? Well, this might be a clue. Your last ten percent might be those times, moments, places, or activities where you have been reluctant to ask God to be present, where you were reluctant to give him that moment as a gift.

Before his conversion, St. Paul was serious about the first ten percent. In fact, I think he gave twenty percent. But when he met Christ, he said, "Jesus doesn't want my first ten percent. He wants my last ten percent." In Galatians 2:20, he says, "I have been crucified with Christ; it is no longer I who live, but Christ who lives in me; and the life I now live in the flesh I live by faith in the Son of God, who loved me and gave himself for me."

Giving the Lord our last ten percent does not lead to burnout. It leads to transformation.

St. Paul learned the secret that Jesus loved us with that last ten percent. So, the question is: Am I going to love him with my last ten percent, or will my life just have a few holy things sprinkled around? Is it just going to be the firstfruits? Am I only going to give God my surplus so that the only things that get transformed are the extra?

If you are willing to give God your ordinary time, your ordinary activities, your ordinary stuff, all the way to the last ten percent, then everything up to the last ten percent sacrificed to the Father becomes extraordinary. Your sacrifice has made it into something sacred. Your life has now become holy.

REFLECT

Discuss an occasion when someone made a sacrifice for you.

What is the role of sacrifice in your life? Who do you find yourself making the most sacrifices for?

One of the precepts of the Church listed in the *Catechism of the Catholic Church* is to help provide for its needs (see CCC 2043). What are your thoughts on this precept?

God wants your last ten percent—that is, a hundred percent of your life. How might you give him your last ten percent this week? What makes you want to hold it back from offering it to him?

Everything we try to keep for ourselves remains ordinary. Only those parts of our lives that are offered to God have the potential to be made holy. What are your thoughts on this?

PRAY

As you pray and meditate on this chapter's message, keep a couple of things in mind. First, don't be daunted by the prospect of offering God your last ten percent. Begin by giving some of yourself *now*, during this moment of prayer. Just "do it now!" Just start. Giving the *last* ten percent begins with giving the *first* ten percent.

Next, make your prayer open-ended. Give ten percent, yes, but be open to giving more, even today! It would be foolish to begin a task without the intention of completing it, and it is the same in our relationship with Christ. Though Jesus wants our all, he welcomes even our smallest gift of self.

As you enter into prayer now, remember the most frequent commandment given in Scripture: "Be not afraid." Our fear of giving God *any* percent of our lives comes from our lack of trust. We think if we give him something, we will be left with less. But this is not how the spiritual life works! As C. S. Lewis notes in *The Screwtape Letters*, God "always gives back to [us] with his right hand what he has taken away with his left."[6]

Just as we cannot swim with one foot on shore or fly without leaving the ground, we cannot experience a deep relationship with Jesus until we willfully let go of our grasp on the things of life. Pray that the Lord will help you increase the percentage of yourself that you can give him today.

ACT

Continuing to be attentive to St. Francis de Sales as a guide, continue to *ask*, *offer*, and *accept* this week. Be particularly attentive to those moments you are reluctant to give to God. These might involve your last ten percent.

CHAPTER 6
GROW AND GUARD

I have always been a fan of heist movies like *The Italian Job* or *Oceans 11*. So I did some research on unbreakable vaults, and I came upon a list of the top ten or fifteen vaults in the world. The vault that tops the list is that of Fort Knox.

The walls of Fort Knox are known as the world's hardest shell. They are made of four-foot-thick granite, 750 tons of reinforced steel, and fireproof material. People estimate that the structure itself could withstand a direct hit from a nuclear bomb. The front doors of Fort Knox are made of twenty-two tons of solid steel. The code that opens the vault is changed every day. No single individual knows the entire code. To open the vault, all authorized individuals must gather to enter the code in the appropriate sequence.

Fort Knox is lined with virtual tripwires and sensors that can detect a passing car, an animal, or a loitering pedestrian in the area. To enter the facility, one must pass a retinal scan, facial recognition, and a thumbprint scan.

A satellite has the entire place under constant surveillance. In some heist movies, there is a camera panning back and forth, and the thieves always make sure that it is not pointing at them when they break into the room. Apparently, there is not one square inch of Fort Knox that is not under a watchful eye from above; there is no dark zone. If someone manages somehow to get past all of this into Fort Knox, its tunnels have a feature that can make them instantly flood to wash away any intruder.

Now, all this security at Fort Knox is to protect the approximately $270 billion worth of gold bars in its vault. During the two world wars, the Magna Carta and the crown jewels of England were stored there for safekeeping. At certain times in history, it also held the Declaration of Independence.

BE ON GUARD

We guard things that have value.

This is nothing new. It goes back to the very beginning. God put Adam and Eve in the Garden of Eden. He gave them the incredible gift of the Garden, saying, in effect, "I give you this to cultivate and to care for. Here's something of value. So you need to cultivate it, grow it, care for it, guard it" (see Genesis 2:15). Whenever we are given something of value, we must cultivate it, grow it, care for it, and guard it.

We have been talking about how God has a vision and a plan for your life. The person that God has made you to be and his place in your life are the things of highest value. So how do you cultivate wonder and gratitude so you can move forward with God's vision for your life right now? Remember, it's not just about the time you spend in church. It is about asking God to be present at every moment. Each moment is a sacrifice you can offer to God—and you can resolve to accept whatever he gives you in that moment. He wants your last ten percent.

Everything we have been talking about relates to how to grow God's vision for your life. Now we are going to talk about guarding this vision. Why? Because we guard valuable things. As Jesus tells us, "Take heed, watch and pray" (Mark 13:33). In other words, be on guard.

Dwayne "The Rock" Johnson has made a name for himself. He had a vision for his life, and it was not just to be another athlete. It was not just to be another wrestler. It was to be a superstar. He went and grew his vision, and now he is a superstar.

Because he is a superstar, we might think that The Rock probably lives it up like the characters he plays in movies. We might assume he stays out late and sleeps in until whenever he wants. That he eats whatever he wants, drinks, and "parties it up."

In reality, though, Dwayne Johnson gets up every morning between three and four a.m. to get a two-hour workout in before he goes to work at six a.m. He works all day, and when he goes home for the day, he doesn't go out. He goes to bed. This is a guy who has a vision for his life, and he has been growing in and guarding that vision.

This is what engaged couples do. They know that their relationship has value, so they seek to grow and guard their love. A Scripture reading often chosen for wedding Masses is Romans 12:9: "Hate what is evil, hold fast to what is good." This means hating whatever can come in between you and your future spouse.

In college, I read the book *A Severe Mercy* by Sheldon Vanauken, a man who grew up in a Christian family but became an atheist. During his junior year of college, he met Jean "Davy" Davis, who was also raised Christian and became an atheist. They soon fell in love.

A Severe Mercy describes their relationship. They dedicated themselves to being what they called "committed pagans." Though they didn't believe in God, they committed their lives to the ideals of truth, goodness, and beauty. They created what they called a "shining barrier" around their relationship, which meant that no one would be able to get in between them. Sheldon and Davy had seen too many of their friends and their parents' friends have their relationships corrupted by others. So they decided to guard their relationship because it was valuable.

Their incredible story goes on. Sheldon began corresponding with C. S. Lewis, and both he and Davy ultimately become Christians. Later in life, Sheldon converts to the Catholic Faith.

Wisdom is knowing what we know from our past, knowing who we are right now, and knowing what God's vision is for our life.

Growing and guarding our vision takes wisdom. We need to know what we need to defend against. Wisdom is knowing what we know from our past, knowing who we are right now, and knowing what God's vision is for our life.

Here's the next step. When it comes to anything, we need to seek wisdom. But many times, we just seek advice. Here's what I mean. Seeking wisdom means going to someone and saying, "Tell me what you know so I can add it to what I know and make a decision." Seeking advice looks like, "Make it easy for me. Tell me what to do."

In Scripture, wisdom is the difference between those who grow and guard God's vision for their lives and those who do not. In Daniel, chapter 12, God makes it clear that all of us end up in one of two places. At one point, we will rise from the dust. There is a resurrection of the dead. Some will rise to an everlasting horror and disgrace, but those who are wise will rise to be like the stars of the sky, to glory.

Someday each of us is going to wake up and realize, *This is the person I have become.* There will be no arguing with it. Either you will have become a wise person from growing and guarding God's vision or not.

EVERY CHOICE MATTERS

Ordinary time is meant to reveal that everything in our lives matters. Every decision makes a difference. None of our moments are really ordinary; they all can be life-changing. As C. S. Lewis puts it, "Every time you make a choice you are turning the central part of you, the part of you that chooses, into something a little different than it was before."[7]

Every time you make a choice, you are turning that central part of you into something a little different. Over the course of your life, you are gradually becoming either a heavenly creature or a hellish one—a person who is in harmony with God, others, and yourself, or one who is in a state of war with God, your fellow creatures, and yourself. And do you know what the Bible calls the central part of you? Your heart.

The *Catechism* describes the heart as "our hidden center, beyond the grasp of our reason and of others; only the Spirit of God can fathom the human heart and know it fully. The heart is the place of decision … It is the place of truth, where we choose life or death" (CCC 2563).

We can guard our time, resources, and relationships because God has a vision for our lives. And if our hearts are so important, we need to guard them too. As Proverbs says, "With all vigilance guard your heart" (4:23, NAB). While we need to guard our time, resources, and relationships, guarding our heart is primary. This is the part of you that chooses. This is the part of you that changes.

> "Only the Spirit of God can fathom the
> human heart and know it fully."
> —CCC 2563

Do you ever feel like your heart is a battlefield? Do you ever feel like you are called to do something but want to do something else instead? Wisdom helps us make decisions with that center part of us at the forefront of our minds—knowing our past, knowing who we are right now, and knowing God's vision for our lives.

The way we guard our hearts might be different from others. Someone could say, "Knowing my past, I rush into relationships too fast. And knowing my present, I'm someone who's been really hurt. Therefore, moving forward, maybe I should be more cautious."

Someone else could say, "Knowing my past, I just don't trust people. And knowing my present, I haven't formed any real relationships because of that lack of trust. Therefore, knowing my future, maybe I should be bolder."

Defending our hearts is going to look different for different people. This is why you don't need advice; you need wisdom.

GUARD YOUR HEART

Scripture gives us four ways we can guard our hearts. We need to guard our hearts with regard to our *words*, our *eyes*, *how we walk*, and *where we find ourselves*.

The book of Proverbs tells us, "Put away from you crooked speech, and put devious talk far from you" (Proverbs 4:24). Now, this obviously has to do with lying, deceitful speech, and gossip. It could also refer to a situation such as revealing everything about yourself to someone you just met.

Next, we are told to "let your eyes look directly forward, and your gaze be straight before you" (Proverbs 4:25). I talk to a lot of people who say, "Father, I was growing. I was pursuing God's vision for my life. And then I thought I could watch that movie, I thought I could go to that website, but it just totally took me out at the knees." If we don't guard our eyes, we are not guarding our hearts.

The third point is to "take heed to the path of your feet, then all your ways will be sure" (Proverbs 4:26). Sometimes we don't watch where we are walking. We are not paying attention to whether we are where God wants us to be or if we are just walking to where we want to go.

Finally, "Do not swerve to the right or to the left; turn your foot away from evil" (Proverbs 4:27). We usually know that something is bad for us, but we choose to do it anyway. One way to guard our heart is to stay away from things that we know are bad for us.

Unlike Fort Knox, guarding our heart is not about locking it up in a vault. At the core, it is about what Proverbs 23:26 presents God saying to each of us: "My [child], give me your heart." So if you want to guard your heart, you need to entrust it to the Lord.

A FATHER'S ADVICE

"Put away from you crooked speech,
      and put devious talk far from you.
Let your eyes look directly forward,
      and your gaze be straight before you.
Take heed to the path of your feet,
      then all your ways will be sure.
Do not swerve to the right or to the left;
      turn your foot away from evil"
(Proverbs 4:24–26).

If you haven't guarded your heart, you won't have it when you need it. This is why almost everything we do as Catholics is about entrusting our hearts to the Father. He keeps our hearts safe so that we can love.

When our hearts are broken because of sin, guilt, and shame, we entrust the broken pieces of our hearts to God in confession. When we read the Bible or hear it proclaimed at Mass, we are entrusting our hearts to God for him to shape and mold them.

> If you want to guard your heart,
> you need to entrust it to the Lord.

One of the ways in which we entrust our heart to God, more than almost any other place, is in the Eucharist. When we receive Holy Communion, we are offering God our heart. And when the Eucharist is placed in our hands, God himself places his heart in our hands.

We entrust our hearts to him, and he entrusts his heart to us. It is an exchange of hearts. *My heart for your heart, God. Now help me grow it. Now help me use it. I'm entrusting it to you. Keep it safe.*

REFLECT

What is the one thing in your life that you value the most? Why is it so valuable to you?

Have you ever lost something because you didn't take the steps to guard or protect it? If you could, what might you do differently?

Growing and guarding takes wisdom—and wisdom comes from experience. Knowing your past, knowing who you are now, and knowing God's vision for your life, what is a way that you can guard God's vision in your life today?

As the *Catechism* notes, "The heart is our hidden center, beyond the grasp of our reason and of others; only the Spirit of God can fathom the human heart and know it fully. The heart is the place of decision, deeper than our psychic drives. It is the place of truth, where we choose life or death. It is the place of encounter, because as image of God we live in relation: it is the place of covenant" (CCC 2563). What resonates with you about this description of the human heart?

Is entrusting your heart to God ever difficult for you? What might be one way you could guard your heart by entrusting it to the Lord today?

PRAY

As the *Catechism* points out, "only the Spirit of God can fathom the human heart and know it fully ... it is the place of covenant" (CCC 2563). Since our heart is the essence of who we are, it is no surprise that we have been called to grow and guard it.

Sometimes, we can let the worries, cares, distractions, and fears of our lives overwhelm our hearts, which can keep us from growing in our relationship with God. "Growing our heart" begins by entering into prayer and asking the Holy Spirit to shine his light on any darkness within, allowing God to heal our hearts and bring us closer to him.

Since we know that our hearts are at risk from the Enemy and circumstances, we must also take them to the Lord for protection. By offering him our innermost being—our heart—we intentionally place ourselves under the protection of his infinitely strong hands. When we do this in prayer, God is sure to show us where and how the Enemy seeks to attack our hearts, making us less likely to fall for his traps.

> *St. Michael the Archangel, defend us in battle. Be our protection against the wickedness and snares of the Devil. May God rebuke him, we humbly pray, and do thou, O Prince of the Heavenly Host, by the power of God, cast into hell Satan and all the evil spirits, who prowl throughout the world seeking the ruin of souls. Amen.*

ACT

This week, be attentive to the ways you are growing and guarding your heart. Write down an area where you need to guard your heart.

REMEMBER

- We need a vision to grow in our character, our relationships with others, and our relationship with God. So that this vision might be more than just a dream, we must stop drifting, and instead come up with a plan of action—and put it into place.

- Most people live a life without wonder. However, in light of God's loving creation and wondrous gift of life, we can grow to see that there are no ordinary moments, no ordinary days, and no ordinary people. Our lives should be filled with wonder!

- Ultimately, we have two options: We can let our lives be defined by their future potential, or by our choices now. The person seeking to become holy does not put things off until later.

- Throughout your day, do these three things: Ask God to be with you, ask for his grace to be present in your life, and then, offer every moment to him.

- If you are willing to give God your "ordinary" time, all the way to the last ten percent, then everything up to the last ten percent sacrificed to the Lord becomes extraordinary. Your sacrifice has made it into something sacred, and your life has now become holy.

- True happiness lies in choosing to grow our hearts closer to God and to guard our hearts from being drawn away from him. We entrust our hearts to him, and he entrusts his heart to us.

NOTES

1   Biographical information about Dietrich Bonhoeffer provided in a homily by
    Fr. Mike Schmitz. For more on Bonhoeffer's life, see "Dietrich Bonhoeffer,"
    The Dietrich Bonhoeffer Institute, tdbi.org.

2   Gilbert Keith Chesterton, *A Short History of England* (London: Chatto and
    Windus, 1917), 59.

3   Chesterton.

4   C. S. Lewis, *The Weight of Glory* (New York: HarperOne, 2001), 46.

5   See Joseph Cardinal Ratzinger (Pope Benedict XVI), *The Spirit of the Liturgy*
    (San Francisco: Ignatius, 2020), 28.

6   C. S. Lewis, *The Screwtape Letters* (New York: HarperOne, 2015), 76.

7   C. S. Lewis, *Mere Christianity* (New York: Macmillan, 1952), bk. 3, ch. 4.

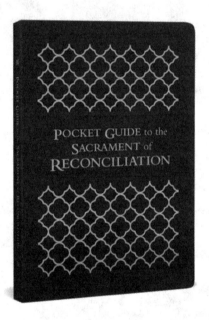